T0055825

SCHIRMER'S LIBRARY
OF MUSICAL CLASSICS

LUDWIG VAN BEETHOVEN

Variations

For the Piano

Edited and Fingered by
HANS VON BÜLOW, SIGMUND LEBERT
AND OTHERS

Translations by
DR. THEODORE BAKER

IN TWO BOOKS

Book I — Library Vol. 6

→ Book II — Library Vol. 7

G. SCHIRMER, Inc.

DISTRIBUTED BY

HAL•LEONARD®
CORPORATION

7777 W. BLUEMOUND RD. P.O. BOX 13819 MILWAUKEE, WI 53213

Contents.
Vol. I.

Nine Variations

on a

March by Dressler

L. van BEETHOVEN.

Printed in the U. S. A.

3

13543

Var.III.

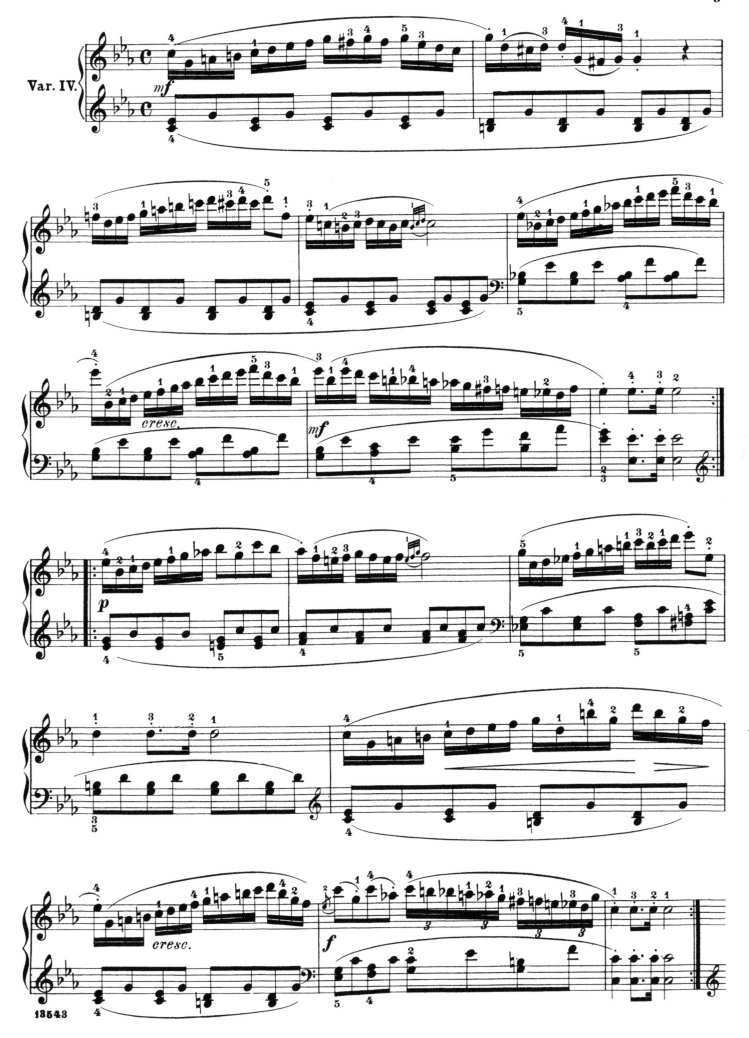

13543

6

Var. V.

13543

Var. VI.

13543

Allegro.

Var. IX.

To Fürst CARL von LICHNOWSKI.

Nine Variations

on the

Theme „Quanto è bello l'amor Contadino.“

from the Opera „La Molinara,“ by Paisiello.

L. van BEETHOVEN.

Var. II.

14

Var. III.

Var. IV. Minore.

13543

Var. VI.

Var. VII.

Tempi di Minuetto.

Var. IX.

Six Variations.

on the Duet

„Nel cor più non mi sento“

from the Opera: „**La Molinara**“ by **Paisiello**.

Edited and fingered by
SIGMUND LEBERT.

L. van BEETHOVEN.

(a) Always strike the appoggiatura-note simultaneously with the first accompaniment-note, somewhat shortly, yet without impairing clearness. The accent falls, however, not on the appoggiatura, but on the principal note.

(b) The alterations given by us in small notes, aim at making these variations easily playable by small hands, which cannot yet stretch an octave.

(c) Continue from this movement to the following without interruption of the measure, except when the contrary is indicated by a fermata over the closing double-bar.

13543

(a) Such a comma indicates a breaking-off somewhat sooner, and a subsequent fresh attack.

(b)

Var. II.

Var. III.

(a) Emphasize the left hand somewhat here, as it has the principal notes of the melody.

(b) Small hands must leave out the lowest tone.

Poco più tranquillo. (♩=144)

Var. IV.

(a) Both the *d - b* in the left hand, as also the *g* in the right, are to be held during the execution of the small notes.

13543

Un pochettino più animato. ($\bullet$ = 60)

Var. VI.

mf sempre legato

(a) *mp* (*mezzo piano*, rather softly) signifies a degree of tone-power between *p* and *mf*

Twelve Variations

on the

Menuet à la Vigano;

from the Ballet "**Le Nozze disturbate**" by **Haibl**.

L. van BEETHOVEN.

30

Var. III.

Minore.

Var. IV.

13543

Maggiore.

Var. V.

Var. VI.

Minore.

Var. VII.

34

Var. IX.

Var. X.

Var. XI.

Var. XII.

Eight Variations

on the

Theme: „Une fièvre brûlante"

from the Opera: "Richard Coeur de Lion" by Grétry.

L. van BEETHOVEN.

13543

41

13543

Var.III.

Var. VI.

Coda.

pp ligato

pp ligato

Presto.

To Gräfin BABETTE von KEGLEVICS.

Ten Variations

on the

Theme: „La stessa, la stessissima"

from the Opera: "**Falstaff**" by **Salieri**.

L. van BEETHOVEN.

Var. II.

Var. III.

Var. IV.

cresc.

Minore.

Var. V.

Var. VII.

Var. VIII.

Allegretto. *(Alla Austriaca.)*

Var. X.

Seven Variations.

on the

Quartet: „Kind, willst du ruhig schlafen"

from the Opera: „**Das unterbrochene Opferfest**" by **P. Winter**.

Allegretto.

L. van BEETHOVEN.

Var I.

Var. III.

Var. V.

Minore.

Var. VI.

Maggiore.

Allegro.

Var. VII

Coda.

Molto allegro.

To Gräfin BROWNE.

Eight Variations

on the

Trio: „Tändeln und Scherzen"

from the Opera: „**Soliman** or **Die drei Sultaninnen**" by **Süssmayr**.

Andante, quasi Allegretto.

L. van BEETHOVEN.

Tema.

Var. I.

13543

Var. III.

Var. IV.

Var. VII.

Molto adagio ed espressivo.

Var. VIII.

Allegro vivace.

Thirteen Variations

on the

Theme: „Es war einmal ein alter Mann"

from the Opera: „**Das rothe Käppchen**" by **Dittersdorf**.

Allegretto.

L. van BEETHOVEN.

Arioso.

Andante con moto.

Tempo I.

Minore.
Espressivo.

Var. VI.

ca-   -lan-   -do   a tempo

ral-   -len-   -tan-   -do

Maggiore.
Allegro non troppo.

Var. VII.

Tempo I.
sempre dolce

Var. VIII.

Con spirito.

Var. IX.

Allegro non tanto, con grazia.

Var. XII.

Capriccio.

Andante.

Marcia vivace.

Var. XIII.

Six easy Variations

on an

Original Theme.

Edited and fingered by
SIGMUND LEBERT.

L. van BEETHOVEN.

(a) ♪ and so, in general, strike all appoggiatur-

as simultaneously with the accompaniment.

(b) The alterations added by us aim at making these variations easily playable by small hands which cannot yet stretch an octave.

(c) By such a comma we indicate that a rhythmical

section must be indicated, and that afterwards a fresh attack must be made.

(d) *mp (mezzo-piano*, rather softly) signifies a degree of tone-power between *p* and *mf*.

(e) Continue from one movement to another without interruption of the measure, except after Variations 3 and 4.

13543

Maggiore.

Tempo I un poco animato. ($\bullet$ = 60)

Var. V.

(a) Emphasize the "melody-bearing" highest part. | (b) Strike ♭ simultaneously with *c*

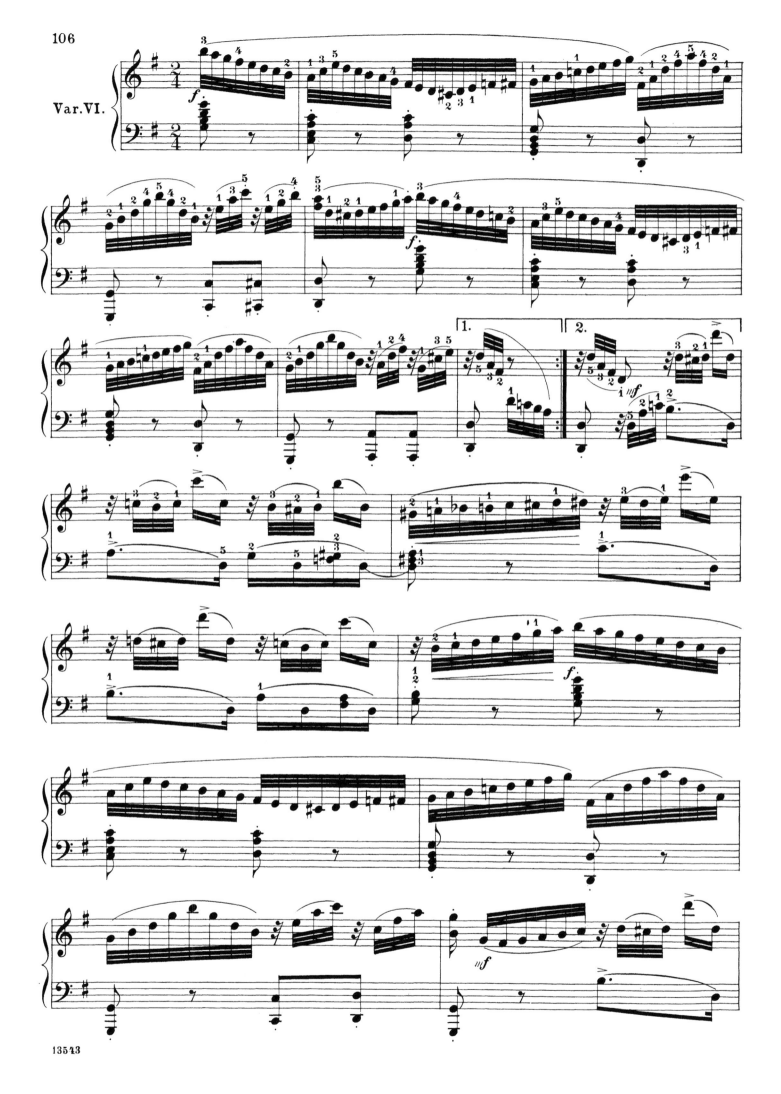

Var.VI.

Coda.
Tempo I.

Six Easy Variations

on a

Swiss Song *)

Edited and fingered by
SIGMUND LEBERT

L. van BEETHOVEN

*) We call special attention to these thoroughly delightful Variations because they are far too little known and appreciated. They will be particularly welcome to *young* pianists.

(a) By a comma we mark those points at which the player ought, by lifting his hands a little earlier than the note-value indicates, to bring out a rhythmical division.

(b) Proceed without interrupting the rhythm; and similarly after Variations 1 and 3.

Minore

Poco sostenuto e doloroso ($\bullet$ = 112)

Var. III

sempre **p** e legato

Maggiore

Tempo I un poco animato ($\bullet$ =126)

Var. IV

legato

Ped. simile

Seven Variations

on the

National Song

"**God save the King.**"

L. van BEETHOVEN.

Tema.

Var. I.

Var. II.

Var. III.

Con espressione.

Allegro:Alla marcia.

Coda.

Adagio.

Allegro.

Five Variations
on the
National Song:
"Rule Britannia."

L. van BEETHOVEN.

Var. II.

Var. V.

Allegro.

Eight Variations

on the

Song:

"Ich hab' ein kleines Hüttchen nur."

L. van BEETHOVEN

Var. III.

Con espressione.

Var. IV.

Var. V.

Var. VII.